# PLEASANT VALLEY SCHOOL

8th grade

Donated by the class of
1962

# PHYSIOLOGY

*JESSIE HELEN HAAG*

*M. VERE DeVAULT*

Illustrated by Marjorie Hart

**THE STECK COMPANY • *PUBLISHERS* • AUSTIN, TEXAS**

# TABLE OF CONTENTS

# INTRODUCTION

Why do I get tired? Why am I hungry at noon? How am I able to do all the things that I do in a day? Why do I stay warm on a cold day? Why can I taste pickles, cherry pie, and salted crackers? What happens to my eyes when I go from a darkened room into the sunlight?

To answer these questions, we must understand how the human body functions. Physiology is the study of the actions of the various parts of our bodies.

4

We know we have muscles, blood vessels, lungs, nerves, stomach, heart, and skin. Each of these organs and tissues has its own job. They work with other parts of our bodies.

If you try the 20 different activities in this book, you may understand some of the ways in which your body works. These experiments can be done at school, at home, by yourself, or with a friend. Why not try them?

# YOUR BODY AND FOOD

*Chewing makes the work of the stomach easier.*

Sometimes we do not chew our food well, and our stomach overworks. Then we get a stomach ache.

Babies have no teeth with which to chew food. Mother gives the baby chopped food so that the work of the stomach will be easier.

Show that chewing food makes the work of the stomach easier.

Get two lumps of sugar. Crush one lump; leave the
other one whole. Place the crushed lump of sugar and
the whole lump in separate glasses of water. Stir and
watch which lump of sugar dissolves more quickly.

*The food tube pushes food into your stomach.*

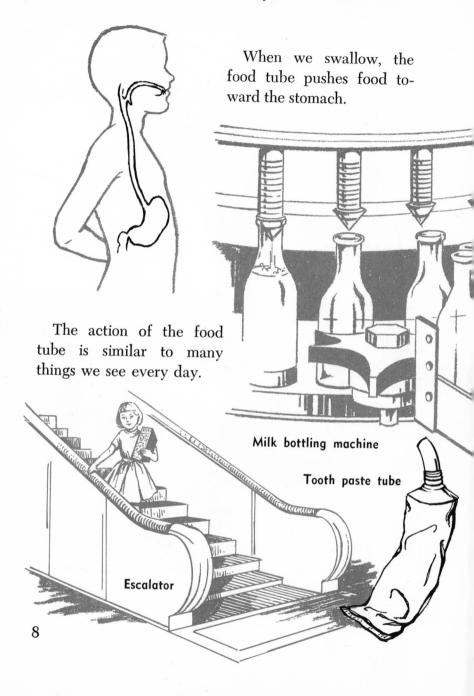

When we swallow, the food tube pushes food toward the stomach.

The action of the food tube is similar to many things we see every day.

Milk bottling machine

Tooth paste tube

Escalator

8

Demonstrate that the food tube pushes food into your stomach.

Have your friend stand on his head. Give him a small piece of celery. Have him chew the celery and swallow it. Does the celery go into the stomach?

*Oxygen is needed to burn food in cells.*

Oxygen is needed for any substance to burn. The oxygen in the air helps keep the bonfire burning.

The fuel in an engine is mixed with air so that it will burn.

Show that oxygen is needed to burn food in cells.

Take a small birthday candle and heat the bottom of the candle to soften it. Stick the soft end of the candle onto a small piece of wood. Float wood in dish of water. Light the candle and cover it with a table glass. Water around the edge of the glass will keep the air, which contains oxygen, from getting to the lighted candle. Does the flame burn for a long time?

*Food produces power.*

During the hour before lunch we are hungry and weak. Our stomach has little food in it. We eat lunch. Food makes us feel strong and powerful again.

Children enjoy a snack in the middle of the morning. This gives them more power to work and play until time for lunch.

Show that heat from burning food in the body produces power.

Take a few tablespoonfuls of popping corn and place them in a covered frying pan. Take a grain of the corn and try to pull it apart. Place frying pan on stove and heat it over a fire. The corn will pop open. The heat produced the power needed to open the grain of corn.

13

# YOUR BREATHING AND PULSE

*Your rate of breathing changes
with your activities.*

Your breathing rate is
slow when you read a book.

Your breathing rate is a
little faster when you climb
stairs.

Your breathing rate is rapid
when you run.

Check to see how your friend's rate of breathing changes.

To check breathing rate, ask your friend to count out loud each time he breathes out. Keep time for one minute.

Check his breathing rate for one minute while:

Resting

Walking

Running

*Your pulse rate changes with your activities.*

Pulse is the force of blood through the arteries. Your pulse rate is steady and slow when you walk leisurely down the street.

Your pulse rate is a little faster when you climb stairs to another floor.

Your pulse rate is very fast when you run to catch a bus.

16

Check to see how your pulse changes with your activities.

1. Can you find your pulse at your left wrist?
2. Check your pulse at different times.
3. Check the pulse for one minute while you are seated.
4. Run for three minutes. Sit down. Check your pulse for one minute.
5. Rest for ten minutes. Check your pulse for one minute while lying down.
6. Check your pulse for one minute while standing.
7. Compare the pulse rates when seated, after running, while lying down, and when standing.

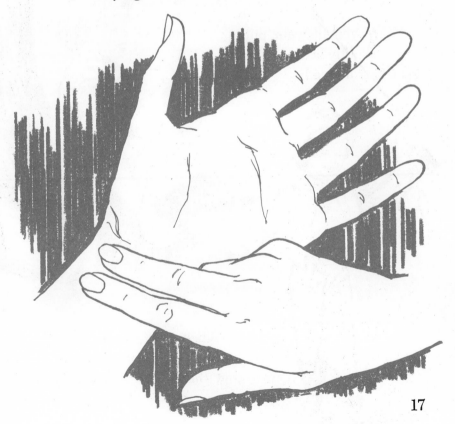

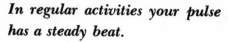

*In regular activities your pulse
has a steady beat.*

When you sleep, your
pulse rate is slow and the
beat is steady.

When you sit, your pulse
rate is slightly faster, but the
beat is still steady.

When you walk, your
pulse rate is even faster,
but the beat is still steady.

18

Check your pulse for a steady beat.

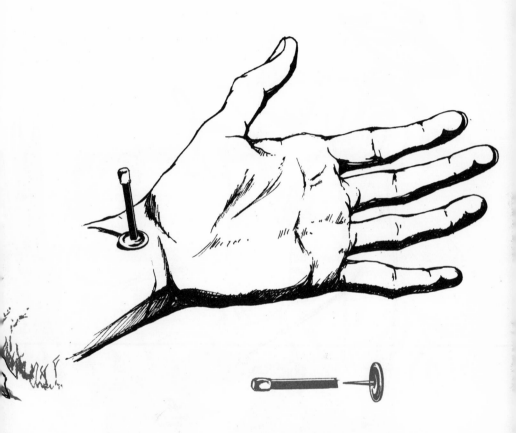

Get a thumbtack and a paper match. Stick the thumbtack into end of paper match. Place the head of the
thumbtack on your pulse at the wrist. Watch the match
bob back and forth.

*Bleeding can be controlled.*

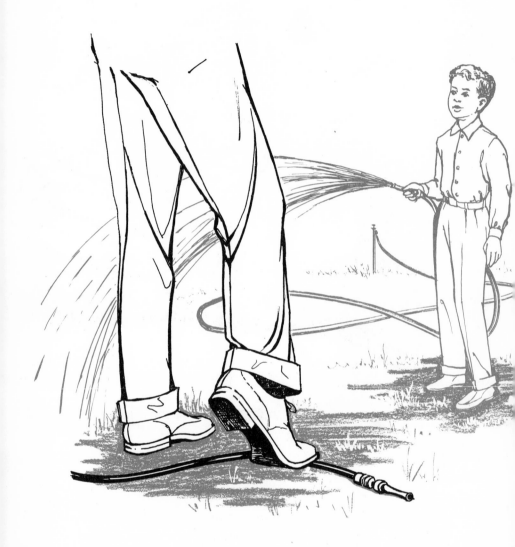

You can stop the flow of water in a soft hose by standing on it.

Control bleeding by putting pressure over the cut.

The next time you cut your finger, place gauze directly over the cut and press hard. What happens?

# YOU TOUCH, SMELL, AND TASTE

*The sense of touch depends upon the location of nerve endings.*

The tailor depends upon his sense of touch as he works with cloth.

The sculptor depends upon his sense of touch as he molds the clay.

Show that the sense of touch depends upon the location of nerve endings.

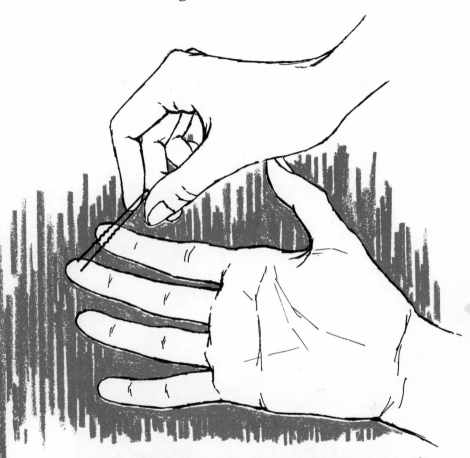

Tell your friend to close his eyes. Take a hairpin with the two points a half inch apart. Have your friend rest his hand on a table, palm up. Touch the tip of one of his fingers with both hairpin points at the same time. Have him tell you if he feels one point or two points. Bring the two points to an eighth of an inch apart. Does he tell you he feels one or two points?

*The sense of smell identifies odors.*

We can smell a good meal cooking.

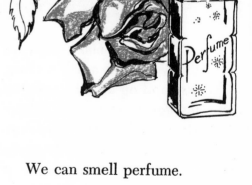

We can smell the roses in the garden.

We can smell gasoline at the service station.

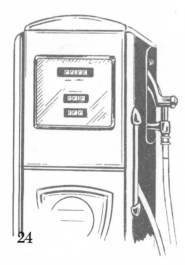

We can smell perfume.

Show that the sense of smell identifies odors.

Blindfold a friend. Select several things to hold under his nose and ask him to smell them and tell what they are. Use a flower, cologne, chocolate, and other objects that have a decided odor.

Sometimes when we first walk into a room we notice a peculiar odor. After awhile the odor seems to go away. Actually the odor is still present. Our sense of smell has only tired of it.

Show that the sense of smell becomes tired.

Blindfold your friend. Hold a pleasant smelling object
such as vanilla, mint, cologne, or perfumed soap under
his nose. Ask him to tell you when you have taken the
object away. Do *not* remove the object. His sense of
smell will become tired, and he will say that it is gone.

The chef in a restaurant and your mother at home try to prepare a meal that smells good. They know that a meal that smells good, tastes good!

Show that sense of smell is stronger than sense of taste.

Blindfold your friend. Cut a thin slice of apple and a thin slice of pear. Place the pear slice under your friend's nose, and put the apple slice into her mouth. Have her tell you what she is eating. Her nose will tell her to say "pear."

29

Some food companies employ people to do nothing but taste the foods they make.

The good chef tastes the food he cooks.

Ice cream companies often invite children to taste their new ice cream flavors.

30

Locate certain taste buds.

Taste buds in different locations on the tongue produce different tastes.

1. Get a pinch of salt, a spoonful of vinegar, a bit of bitter tasting stuff (coffee), and a pinch of sugar. Have a clean toothbrush handy.
2. Dip the toothbrush in water. Touch it to the salt. Touch the brush to the tip of your tongue. Is it salty?
3. Take a mouthful of water and rinse your mouth. Clean the brush. Dip the brush in the vinegar. Touch the brush to the tip of your tongue. Is it sour? Touch the brush to the sides of the tongue. Is it sour?
4. Take a mouthful of water and rinse the mouth. Clean the brush. Dip the brush in the coffee. Touch the brush to the tip, sides, and back of tongue. Where did it taste bitter?
5. Take a mouthful of water and rinse the mouth. Clean the brush. Dip the brush in the sugar. Touch the brush to the tip of tongue. Is it sweet?

# TEAMWORK OF NERVES AND MUSCLES

*The nerves of both eyes and
all muscles work together.*

A basketball player and
other athletes need eyes and
muscles that work well together.

Father needs eyes and
muscles that work well together when he drives the
car.

Mother needs eyes and
muscles that work well together when she cooks and
sews.

Illustrate some situations in which nerves of both eyes and all muscles work together.

1. Lace one shoe or put one sock on as you stand on the opposite foot. Do not support yourself.

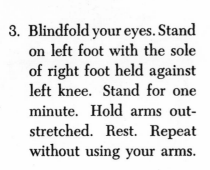

2. In your right hand hold the cap of a fountain pen. In your left hand hold the rest of the fountain pen, point up. Straighten your left arm. Close one eye. Place the cap on the pen in one quick movement. Can you do it?

3. Blindfold your eyes. Stand on left foot with the sole of right foot held against left knee. Stand for one minute. Hold arms outstretched. Rest. Repeat without using your arms.

# SKIN KEEPS YOU BOTH WARM AND COOL

*Your skin is a covering of warmth.*

A swimmer's skin helps keep him warmer than the water in which he swims.

When you take a cold shower, your skin helps keep you warmer than the water.

Show that your skin is a covering of warmth.

Use a regular household thermometer. What is the temperature of the room? Tuck the thermometer under your armpit. Leave it there for two minutes. What temperature does the thermometer show?

*Sweat glands pour water on the skin to cool it.*

When a basketball player stops playing, he is covered with sweat. To avoid cooling too rapidly he wears a jacket.

When the farmer finishes heavy work in the field, he should put on a jacket.

Illustrate that water on the skin cools the skin.

Take a small piece of absorbent cotton. Dip the cotton into warm water. Place the wet cotton on your wrist. How does your wrist feel?

# YOUR FOOT

*A foot is like a bridge.*

Weight on a single board across a ditch is distributed between the ends.

The weight on some bridges is distributed between the ends of the bridge.

Show that your foot is like a bridge.

The weight of your body is distributed between the base of the toes and the heel.

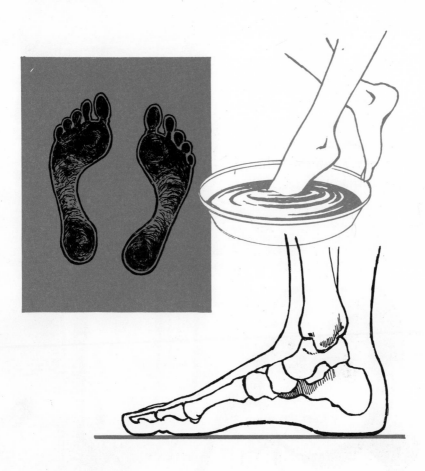

Remove your shoe and sock. Dampen the sole of your foot with water. Step upon brown wrapping paper. Trace the outline of your footprint. What parts of the foot support the weight of your body?

# THE IRIS—"WINDOW SHADE" OF THE EYE

*The iris regulates the amount of light going into the eyeball.*

When we first go into a darkened theatre, we cannot see too well. A few minutes later, we can see other people sitting near us.

When we go out-of-doors after the show, the light is too bright for our eyes.

Check to see that the iris regulates the amount of light going into the eyeball through the pupil.

Go into a dimly lighted room and look at your eyes in a mirror. Notice the size of the colored iris. Go to a lamp with the shade off. Turn on the light and look into the mirror. Watch the change that takes place in the size of the pupil.

# FATIGUE IN MUSCLE ACTION

*Irregular muscle action tires the muscle more quickly than a steady muscle action.*

The untrained typist tires easily. Her movements are jerky and uneven.

The experienced typist works steadily and quickly. She can work many hours without tiring.

Demonstrate that irregular muscle action tires the muscle more quickly than a steady muscle action.

Tap a piano or typewriter key jerkily, irregularly, and quickly. Use one finger. Do not use any wrist or other finger movement. Stop when tired and time yourself. Rest for two or three hours. Now tap slowly and evenly. Continue as long as you can and time yourself. Compare the lengths of time.

# SUMMARY

During this study of physiology, you have learned some ways your body works. You have completed 20 different activities. These should help you better understand why your body works the way it does.

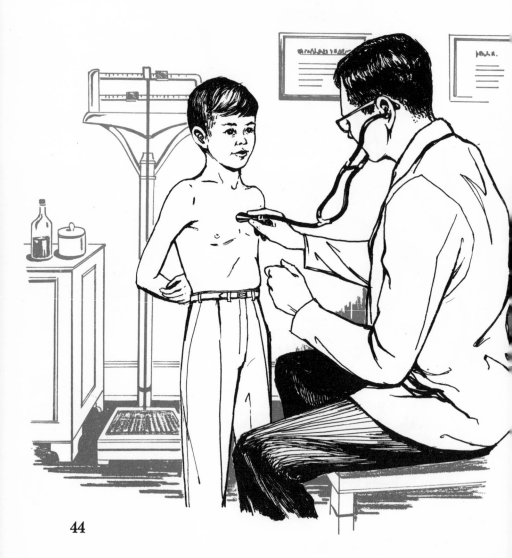

The first group of things you tried showed you how your body uses food. You found that:

1. Chewing food makes the work of the stomach easier.
2. The food tube pushes food into your stomach.
3. Oxygen is needed to burn food in cells.
4. Heat from burned food in our body produces power.

The second group of activities told you how the pulse rate changes with your activities and how bleeding can be controlled.

The third group of experiences gave you a chance to discover the jobs of the organs of taste, touch, and smell.

The fourth group of things you tried showed how the nerves of both eyes and muscles work together.

In the fifth group of activities you discovered that your skin is a covering of warmth and that it also keeps you cool.

The sixth group of experiences proved that your foot is like a bridge because the weight of your body is distributed between the base of the toes and the heel.

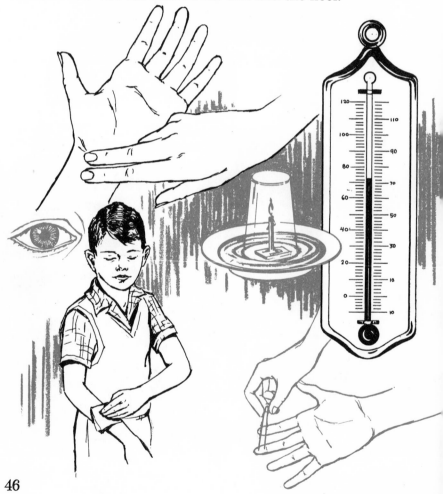

During the seventh group of things you tried you found the answer as to how your eyes regulate the amount of light going into the eyeball.

The eighth group of activities showed you that irregular muscle action makes you tired more quickly than steady muscle action.

What other things can you do that will show the functions of other parts of the human body?